Your Safe Haven

Merrel Ya

Ukiyoto Publishing

All global publishing rights are held by

Ukiyoto Publishing

Published in 2023

Content Copyright © Merrel Ya

ISBN 9789358462425

All rights reserved.
No part of this publication may be reproduced, transmitted, or stored in a retrieval system, in any form by any means, electronic, mechanical, photocopying, recording or otherwise, without the prior permission of the publisher.

The moral rights of the author have been asserted.

This is a work of fiction. Names, characters, businesses, places, events, locales, and incidents are either the products of the author's imagination or used in a fictitious manner. Any resemblance to actual persons, living or dead, or actual events is purely coincidental.

This book is sold subject to the condition that it shall not by way of trade or otherwise, be lent, resold, hired out or otherwise circulated, without the publisher's prior consent, in any form of binding or cover other than that in which it is published.

www.ukiyoto.com

*To the quiet ones who grew up
in fear, insecurities, and doubts.*

We all need a safe haven: a place to be vulnerable, to hide, to lament, to sing, and to heal. These are collections of journals, poems and letters about life, love, faith, failures, and struggles that we all face. Beautiful reminders to uplift you and remind you that you are ***not fighting hard battles alone***.

This is your safe haven, a time to seek silence and listen to the noise raging inside your heart and give you a safe space to freely break down at heaven's gate and pour out your emotions. This is your haven telling you, you should liberate yourself from the thoughts that constantly imprison you. This is your safe space, reminding you that it is time to heal and break the bondage of fear. This is your safe space reminding you that it is time to inhale His grace once again. This is your safe space, reminding you to bring back the little kid inside you who lives in faith and not by sight and pursues love more than fears and doubts. This is your safe space reminding you to forgive the ones who caused pain to you when you were younger and to flee from the cage of fears and doubts. This is your safe haven, embracing your wounds from the past and giving you space to heal at your own pace. This is your safe haven hoping to see you at the peak of the mountain dancing instead of screaming, celebrating instead of lamenting, and winning instead of losing.

Have a quiet time to listen to the inner voice you have muzzled for a long time, feelings and fears you have suppressed, wounds you constantly hide, and dusty dreams and hopes inside your closet. Have a quiet time and allow yourself to rekindle your hopes, dreams, and passion. Have a quiet time to say the words you want to say to yourself but you always neglect. Have a quiet time to listen to the longings you do not utter to anyone and the love you wish you had once. Have quiet time to choose a life full of meaning instead of regrets. Have a quiet time and loosen your grip on the things that constantly hurt you.

To the tired ones, lost, lonely, afraid, and confused; this is your haven. As you go along the pages, get a pen and pour out your heart and may you find the healing that your soul needs. Read this one day at a time so you can digest each page. Have a quiet walk, a quiet time, and a quiet talk to yourself, venture into the intricate pattern of your soul, and find the true meaning of life, your purpose. You will find yourself when you seek God first. You can always trust the Author of life, the Giver of life, and the Great Storyteller.

Merrel Ya

Keep journals.
Your journey is in your journal.
Your journey is your story.
Your story has a purpose.

Merrel Ya

Contents

Day 1: Life	1
Day 2: Calmness	4
Day 3: Quiet Walk	7
Day 4: Slow Morning	10
Day 5: When You Feel Blue	13
Day 6: It's really okay! Okay?	16
Day 7: Happiness	19
Day 8: Self-care	22
Day 9: Self-love	25
Day 10: Smile	28
Day 11: Safe Space	31
Day 12: Your Life Is A Blessing	34
Day 13: Genuine Connection	37
Day 14: Forgiveness	40
Day 15: Prisoners	43
Day 16: Delays	46
Day 17: Growing Up	49
Day 18: Waiting	52
Day 19: Try Again	55
Day 20: When It's Hard To Dream	58
Day 21: Hey, Just Show Up!	61
Day 22: Gratitude	64
Day 23: Faith Over Fear	67

Day 24: Fallen And Broken	70
Day 25: Healing	73
Day 26: On Brokenness	76
Day 27: Before You Lose Hope	79
Day 28: Restoration	82
Day 29: Kind Love	87
Day 30:_____	90
Someone Out There	92
On Love	93
Can You Faithfully Wait?	94
Step Back	95
If	96
Letters For Your Longing Heart	997
About the Author	*120*

Day 1: Life

Life will teach you many things if you remain open to the possibilities, improbabilities, corrections, detours, and even suffering. The beauty, the mundane, and the mystery. Welcome sadness and happiness, the highs and the lows, the compliments and criticisms, the sentiments and judgments, the love and hate, the affection and rejection, the success and failures; the irony of life itself. The people who will come and the people you need to let go. Be open to the irresistible pain and to the unequivocal joys and meanings. Life is whimsical, remain open to what life throws and practice detachment from the world, express and never suppress, love and serve passionately, and enjoy life at its best. Again, do not fixate; practice detachment to the things that will not last, things you will not bring when you are six feet below the ground. Shut the noise around and discover the intricate pattern of life: your voice, your story, and your purpose. Listen to the One who lives in you because every one of us will give an account of our lives. Choose life, choose to wander in the intricate pattern of the universe, and see how beautiful it is to live under His grace.

*Life is full of tests yet full of **purpose**.*
*Full of revisions yet full of **meanings**.*
*Full of distractions yet full of **peace**.*
*Full of emptiness yet full of **provisions**.*
*Full of failures yet full of **promises**.*
*Full of mistakes yet full of **Grace**.*
*His **love** is beyond measure.*

What is the most important thing you've learned in life so far?

Day 2: Calmness

I hope you learn to love the things that don't cost much. The birds singing hymns, the puffy clouds following your way to your dreams, the sun shining brightly while its rays penetrate your body and warm your soul. Inhale the aroma of hope as you sip your coffee at the kitchen sink. Go for a walk, a quiet walk. Enjoy the tranquillity and solemnity of life. The world is noisy; find a wide space where you can meet your true self with no big expectations, forget your frustrations, and dream with full determination.

Breathe deeply, then continue.

Do not worry about tomorrow because tomorrow will worry about itself. Do not forget to grab the lamp when it's dark, then take it easy and watch your step. The lamp lights every step you take and does not light the next path, so you can focus on where your feet are. Surely the light is enough until you reach the end of the tunnel. If you get disheartened as you meet hard people, never forget to forgive and remove all the layers of hate, anger, and sadness creeping inside; these might kill your beautiful soul as they can turn you into a person you are not. If you get frustrated as conflicts and trials arise, never forget to highlight them because they add colors and hues to the grey spaces of your life. All these struggles are for nothing.

You can always choose calmness in your messiness.

*Calmness is a superpower that many people disregard.
Calmness never hides and is always available around.
In the loud snores, loud cries, loud frustrations, and
loud disappointments.
When everything falls apart, it is easier to wail in anger,
You can always use your power to find tranquility amid
calamity.*

Your Safe Haven

What makes you calm and rested? List it down and do it more often.

Day 3: Quiet Walk

Sometimes all you need is just a quiet walk. Allow yourself to reconnect with your soul, even in a mundane space. Not running or chasing, just let your feet walk and absorb the simplicity and complexity of life so you can be grateful again. Sometimes all you need is a quiet walk, allowing yourself to look beyond the surface of life and see the heart and soul of each individual. Sometimes all you need is a quiet walk, allowing yourself to sit in silence and find inspiration from the people around you for showing up each day and giving you the courage to do the same.

Walking is therapeutic for me. It is looking beyond what the eyes can see and unraveling the deep truths of life. That all people are trying to get up and fight for their lives, having small talks with the street vendors about how beautiful it is to live with deep contentment and not ask for more, having good conversations with professionals inspiring you to dream bigger, sitting down with the little ones and playing with them and make you forget the inflation rate, seeing the beggar begging for food, seeing homeless walking with their bare feet living in the fullness of joys, and seeing yourself gazing at the clouds and appreciating how big the world is and how beautiful it is to live and to dream bigger, despite of its irony.

Have a quiet walk and list down your random thoughts here.

Day 4: Slow Morning

You need a slow morning, not rushing and chasing, simply sitting, walking, listening, roaming, absorbing, and taking time. It is sipping your coffee with gladness and joy, unafraid of what is next, and unapologetic for the way you exist. It is playing under the sun, asking His grace to penetrate you, loving yourself the way He loves you, finding peace in uncertainties, doing what ignites your soul, leaving the past behind, and living in the present moment. Be present in the slow morning, experiencing silence, solitude, and stillness, escaping a few seconds in the routines of life, appreciating the simplicity and complexity of each morning, and realizing that you are still here, *breathing*.

Everyone is in haste, afraid to waste split seconds. Slow days and slow mornings seem like a burden and baggage. But may you give yourself a favor? Can you please slow down for a moment? Can you accommodate your soul for just few minutes? Can you sit in silence and thank God? Take a rest.

Wake up at 5 am and enjoy your slow morning. Describe what you see and what you feel.

Day 5: When You Feel Blue

Beloved, it is okay to feel blue even though the sky is purple. You do not need to defend yourself from other people who constantly make you feel less and small. They do not know who you are and your entire story and do not require yourself to listen to them. Instead of listening to lies, pour out your heart to God. He is with you all along. He understands you because He knows you better than anyone else. He understands you simply because He created you. He never ignores your feelings, so keep doing what He asks you to do, not for others but for Him and for the ones who might need it. Don't let other people control your feelings. Be Spirit-filled.

Sadness, frustration, and discouragement come and go. Feel, but learn to let go. Cry in anger, but do not sink in pain. You are not your feelings and emotions. You are beautiful, loved, seen, and heard. When others hurt you, please do not absorb their heartaches instead, listen to their wounds and pray for their healing.

It is okay to cry when loneliness resides and hopelessness seems so close. Write anything you want to say here.

Day 6: It's really okay! Okay?

You are not everyone's cup of tea.

It is okay to be misunderstood and to be different.

It is okay to go against the flow, not to follow the norm or the crowd, and not to desire the glow of the limelight.

It is okay to deploy some detachments from people's point of view of you, not attracting attention when everyone wants it, and not waiting for validation and affirmation from others. You can create more space for all the parts of you: your imperfections, flaws, weaknesses, and limitations, and allow His power to work within you and change you.

Stop striving to fit in when your design is to set apart because your purpose is to reflect His light.

Stop trying to force yourself to sit at the table, you are not welcome.

Consider that you are always invited to sit at the Master's table.

To the quiet ones, please remember not to dim your light.
You do not need to be loud just to be bold.
Your quiet spirit, gentleness, and tenderness
deserve a space here.
You are supposed to illuminate His light and radiate around
and fill the dark spaces purposely designed for your light.
Please show up and make your light visible.

Why do you constantly dim your light?

Day 7: Happiness

Happiness is everywhere.

You can find it in the kitchen sink while washing the dirty plates while sipping your coffee in the morning with your messy hair and baggy clothes. You can find it in the grocery store while picking up the food you always wanted when you were just a little kid. You can find it at your office while pouring your heart as you finish all your reports. You can find it while walking at the park and sitting on the grass while eating ice cream worth twenty pesos. You can find it in the stars at night, dancing to the melody of your favorite music, and imagining the best scene at your wedding. You can find it as you look in the mirror while accepting your imperfections and embracing your small wins each day. You can create happiness and transcend it to other people. You can use your creativity and inspire yourself and others. You can find it in the little things, in the most unremarkable moments of life.

Find happiness in the ordinary, in the mundane days, in seemingly unremarkable moments, even in the hard seasons, and even at the peak of your success. Happiness is always within you.

List all the little things that makes you happy. Do it more often.

Day 8: Self-care

Practice self-care. Give space and grace to yourself as well. Make sure you are nourishing yourself as well. You cannot pour out the water in an empty cup. Be kinder to yourself. You do not need to travel or go to different places to do self-care, do what makes you happy, and do what makes you calm and rested. Sometimes it is just a quiet walk, a good book or movie, a song, or simply gazing at the trees and enjoying the simplicity and complexity of life. Taking care of yourself is productivity. Solitude finds gratitude.

Remember to nourish not only your body but also your mind, heart, and soul. Go on a library date with yourself and sit silently in one corner while reading your favorite book. Then, ride on a bus, and walk into the park while sipping your coffee and enjoying the mundane day. Make sure not only to include glorious adventure in your story but don't forget those simple moments that make you alive. Self-care is when you fill your heart with so much joy and peace and when you choose to live fully rather than half-heartedly. Enjoy the fullness of life.

Pamper yourself today. Do the things that nourish your heart, mind, body, and soul. Describe what you feel after doing those things.

Day 9: Self-love

Loving yourself should not be a burden. If you do not like the person you represent or you do not like what you see in the mirror- dehypnotize yourself from false beliefs. Perhaps you absorb it from others unknowingly. There is one person for you who will validate you when everyone does not: the one who will love you when you are the hardest person to love, the one who understands the intricate pattern of your soul, the one who cherishes your inmost being, and the one who gives space for your failings and mistakes and you should always see that person in the mirror. May you love yourself deeply and profoundly so you can give love to others as well. You are loved just the way you exist. Embrace your innermost being, the parts of you that you do not like to post on social media, your flaws, limitations, and imperfections that you constantly hide; strive to be better despite those. Say all the kind words you always long to hear. And above all, may you always see yourself as God sees you: favored, loved, chosen, forgiven, strong, hopeful, and faithful. Do something that best represents Christ. When you start loving Christ, surely you will start loving yourself as well as the people around you.

Loving yourself is not self-seeking. Loving yourself deeply is loving others as well deeply and profoundly. Taking care of yourself is the most beautiful gift you can offer to others because you can give your very best because you know yourself very well. Loving yourself is having the courage to venture into the intricacies of life. Loving yourself is being joyful with small wins and appreciating the person you see in the mirror. It is when you know how to validate and affirm your inmost being without expectation from other people to do it for you. It is forgiving yourself as always instead of belittling yourself, choosing self-confidence over self-pity, and choosing faith instead of unbelief. It is seeing yourself whole because your worth comes from Christ alone.

List all the things you love most about yourself.

Day 10: Smile

The world needs your smile, a glimpse of hope for someone's weary soul. Have you ever noticed that living becomes harder each day? All of us have baggage to carry, but you can be the person who always choose hope. Some stay on their deathbed right now, fighting for their lives and hoping to have more days, and here you are standing still despite all the circumstances. So choose to smile even if your shoulders are tired and your feet are weary. Keep smiling. Life is still beautiful: the sun shines every day, the moon and stars light up our dark sky, the trees dance in slow motion, and the birds are still flying high. Do not forget to enjoy life because you only have one. Smile and let it radiates around your space!

Smile you will look ten times younger.

Smile that is your ticket to your dreams, to the palace, and to your lover.

Smile, be tender, and be gentle in this world full of toughness and roughness.

*Capture your best smile today and paste here.
Have a positive self-talk.*

Day 11: Safe Space

Life is already hard. There are a lot of pressures and disappointments around. May you find the people who could be your safe space and your escape place. It is okay if they are just one or two. If you find them, you do not need to try hard just to be accepted. They always make you feel at home. They always welcome you with a loving embrace despite your weaknesses and celebrate your small wins. You can wear your favorite dress even if it's polka-dots. You can cry even at the smallest things and share your loudest laugh. You are deeply loved just the way you are, the way you exist. Life is already hard. May you find the people who won't make it harder and make your burdens lighter.

Your safe space should start in you. When you finally accept your limitations and weaknesses and strive to be better instead of remaining little, you will find people with the same amount of patience and generosity within themselves, people with the same love for themselves. Everyone gives because everyone is full of love. No one is begging, no one is asking, and everyone is giving because love, acceptance, and forgiveness are overflowing.

*Describe the people who make you feel at home
and be that kind of person to everyone.*

Day 12: Your Life Is A Blessing

Your life is a blessing to someone else. Someday you will be glad because you keep the faith, you choose to persevere, and you choose to hope. Perhaps you never know that some people look at you and admire your courage, your faith, and your perseverance. Those young minds who stare at you whenever you pass by on the road, hoping to be like you in the future. God can use your story of failures, defeats, and heartaches to glorify His name when you choose to show up even in your struggles and you never know you might encourage others to do the same. Your little light could still light up a dark life once you choose to reflect His light.

"God is proud of you," someone told me. I will not forget that. I want you to know that God loves to see His children becoming His blessings to other people as well. God loves to bless you so you can be His vessel, just be faithful with the little things He entrusted you because surely He will trust you even in great things ahead.

Ask your favorite buddy to write something here that best describes you.

Day 13: Genuine Connection

We all want genuine connection, but living in this generation teaches us to wear masks to protect ourselves from coming to one another, to hide parts of us we don't like, and constantly find imperfections and faults in being ourselves. Living in this generation that diagnoses every little thing of our actions and mistakes, *there is something wrong with you.* Thus, many of us are trying hard to be someone we are not, afraid of failing, afraid of trying and making mistakes, and scared of being human. It is hard to pursue genuine connections if we are not being true to ourselves. It requires authenticity, vulnerability, sincerity, and accountability. Easier said than done.

Living in this digital space where everything is perfectly artificial yet superficial. May you build genuine connections: small talks about life and deep conversations about purpose, love, struggles, and passion. More soulful, more human.

Connect to someone today and ask about his or her aspirations, favorite food, life lessons, or anything under the sun that would make the other person feel valued and appreciated. Write the things you've learned in your conversation.

Day 14: Forgiveness

Forgive yourself for committing mistakes and failures instead of beating yourself. Forgive others and give grace as well. You are not greater than when others commit mistakes to you; in the same manner, you are not less than when you commit mistakes to others. Life is more beautiful when you remove all the hate, anger, frustrations, and disappointments inside your heart. Life is more beautiful when you choose to forgive and love. Move forward because there's so much more ahead of you.

Do you know why this world is full of broken people and unhealed ones? Because most people suppress and hide. They keep their feelings and emotions sealed in a box full of frustrations, anger, fears, unbelief, hurt, and hate. Not knowing they are self-inflicting, the scratch turns into deep wounds until it causes pain to others. Forgive yourself, open the box, and express and never suppress, so you will find yourself full of grace and able to forgive others.

Forgive yourself so you can forgive others too.
Use the space to reconcile with yourself.

Day 15: Prisoners

The world has enough spokesperson for loneliness, pain, and heartache and prisoners of fears and doubts. May you become the person who speaks light, beauty, and faith. May you become a prisoner of hope instead of fear, a spokesperson of joy instead of loneliness. May you become the one who walks by faith instead of unbelief so you will love yourself in a way you do not want to be like any other person, you will love your story in a way that you dare not to follow anyone else's dreams, you will love His Word that you do not want to follow the flow of this world.

Do you want to liberate yourself? Get out of your cage, from your fears, pride, discontentment, disappointment, unbelief, unforgiveness, hate, jealousy, entitlement, and all this unrighteousness of your flesh that imprison you from the life that God wants you to experience, a life full of meaning: life with peace, joy, hope, forgiveness, kindness, generosity, patience, goodness, and faithfulness.

What are the things that constantly imprison you?

Day 16: Delays

Delays are beautiful in this world full of instants. May you have the courage to wait intently, patiently, courageously, and actively. It is purposely part of life. It takes a full season for fruit to mature and ripen. Sometimes you worry so much about how fast you will get there, but God is concerned about how strong you grow and how firm your faith is. The pauses on your journey would help you in your growth. Just remain faithful, plant the seeds, pour your heart into it, and watch it grow. We work and God blesses us with the fruits, so it is okay if you are experiencing delays. Perhaps you are prioritizing your goals and delaying your wants. You might be prioritizing your family and delaying your desires, prioritizing your growth and delaying your comfort, or prioritizing your studies and delaying your beats. You will reap what you sow; for every cause, there is an effect. Endure and enjoy those delays!

Some things are beyond your control. Those delays might be impulses of warnings to take rest and pause. Listen, if the universe allows you to experience delays in the middle of strange situations and unexpected transitions. Look around, pause, and wonder. Those delays might mean something greater which you can ponder.

Perhaps there is something more on the flip side of delays. It might not be a better opportunity. Instead, the delays make you a better version of yourself so your feet will remain on the ground. Take this time to express your gratitude.

Day 17: Growing Up

When you were young, it was so cool growing up. It was fun to be in different places and meet new people; it was easier to make mistakes and cover up, and it was exciting to face uncertainties, but now growing up means trying to be in a situation you have never expected and dreamed of and facing realities in times of uncertainty. There are moments you feel terrible; unable to wake up, get up, and show up. It is hard to be vulnerable and show all your unspoken aches and cries. It is hard to explain to your parents that your aspirations fall into pieces and hopes suddenly vanish; **this transition of hurting, breaking, and weeping.** You have disheartening moments in your bedroom with your knees in deep prayers, in the comfort room of your workplace unable to breathe, and in the street with your weary feet unable to find your way home.

Sometimes your **breakthrough** *is not the most ideal and sensible one and not the one that you see in the movie or the highlight reel of people on social media. It is when you do not have anything but your* **faith in Him***. It is when you feel lost but you find* **the way in Him***. It is when you feel scared, but* **His presence** *gives you peace. Your greatest breakthrough is knowing that you are inadequate to save yourself. It is knowing and believing you always need* **Jesus** *in all the days of your life.*

How are you lately?

Day 18: Waiting

Maybe you've been waiting for a long time, maybe you've been persevering and doing the hard work for a long time, and you still haven't seen the fruits of your labor. All of your tears at night have already soaked your trust. You might not notice it, but you are certainly more courageous in this life. The person you are becoming is more significant than the things you constantly wish for. He certainly does not forget your petitions, and He is aware of all your efforts for Him. Remember, if you labor, you work; if you pray, God works. Rest your heart, it will all make sense eventually. There is an effect for every cause. What you seed is what you will reap.

Waiting is also part of your story and you never waste time when you choose to wait for God to answer. Choose to wait for great things you always long for and always work for. After all, you will reap what you sow in due season. Just be faithful. Your faithfulness always results in fruitfulness. His grace is enough.

What are you waiting for? Who are you waiting for? Why are you waiting? Write and tell to God.

Day 19: Try Again

Allow yourself to try again when you fail and falter. You can create a space for failures, mistakes, and disappointments you hold to yourself. Don't suppress your emotions, feel them, and slowly let them go. Don't invalidate yourself others will do that. You can start and try again. Don't absorb other people's feelings and opinions about you because you know yourself better than they do. Not everyone in your life will understand your courage to become better each day. You are making progress. You can stop when you get tired and confused but never go backward. Stop and take one step forward. We learn and grow differently, choose your pace, choose what's best for you. Listen to the ones who calm your heart and give you enough peace. Try again, but this time try with God because He is able.

Just try again.

You never know the possibility of failing so as to win.

Just try again.

You never really know you are just one step closer to your dream.

Just try again.

You never really know you're halfway closer to the palace.

Just try again.

You never really know you're already one inch closer to your lover.

And even if not, you won't know if you haven't even tried.

So why not try again? Have you ever forgotten?

God is with you.

List all the things you want to do if you are ten times bolder.

Day 20: When It's Hard To Dream

I hope you remember the little kid inside you who lives in faith and not by sight and who pursues love more than fears and doubts. I hope you remember that your faithfulness results in fruitfulness. I hope you remember that your Father desires success in your purpose. I hope you remember that all your God-given dreams will happen because it is for His glory. Allow mistakes and failures to come around, but don't let in those dream killers. Risk-takers don't do the same thing. If you succeed, you will be happy you did it and if you fail, you will be wiser. Pursue what ignites your soul. Choose His path. Endure the valley of disappointments, ingrain in the process, and the mundane days. Enjoy the ride, be happy, and take heart.

Your dream is a fire burning deep within that ignites your soul, a passion committed to a bigger purpose, and gives you so much motivation to add meaning to this cruel world, to make the world a better place. Get up, look up, and give yourself a favor to dream and make it happen.

What stops you from pursuing the dreams He put inside your heart?

Day 21: Hey, Just Show Up!

Showing up means persevering and surrendering. Your effort is not in vain. You will fail, but He will constantly give you the strength to believe and to persevere. Plant a prayer now, plant your goals, and pursue them with courage. Plant your dreams with your knees and let Him guide you through the process. If you are working for Him, He will sustain you. Whatever your hands find to do, do it will all your might and do it for His glory. He will give you strength, wisdom, courage, and perseverance when you are tired and disheartened. Your part is to show up, persevere, and surrender. Surely you will reap what you sow. You will harvest the fruits of your hard work in due season. Do not let those dream killers kill your passion and purpose. Instead, listen to the One who put the desires in your heart.

Just show up even if your legs are trembling,
and even if you are stuttering.
You'll get there too, and you'll make it too.
But first dare to be seen and to be heard. Testify!

***Write the triggers that cause you not to show up.
Pray for them.***

Day 22: Gratitude

If you are worried about life's difficulties, sit down at the corner and write something you are grateful for today or look at your life ten years ago. Give thanks and slow down your attention; soak in the moment. Instead of counting all accomplishments and material things you have and do not have, gaze at the person you see right now, more confident, secure, hopeful, and courageous. Count all the good things happening in your life until you realize there are ten thousand reasons to be thankful.

Having a life here is already a win.

If you can still sing, sing out loud even if you're out of tune. If you can dance, dance even if you can't go along with the beats. If you can still jump, jump high. If you can still dream, dream beyond the surface level. If you can still love, love even the unlovable. If you can still write, write all the stories inside your soul. If you can still hope, hope for a better future. You are in a constant win when you are breathing. Remember His breath fills your lungs. When your oxygen suddenly depletes you will realize how beautiful it is to live here, how beautiful it is to have strength: to walk, to jump, to venture into different places, you will realize how beautiful it is to see beautiful things around: the sky, the clouds, the stars, and the moon. So breathe because tomorrow is never a promise. Celebrate your life. You are still here. Celebrate your time here, rejoice in the Lord.

Be grateful.

Look for the little things that you are so grateful for.

Day 23: Faith Over Fear

We all wrestle from fear of judgment, rejection, and failure. Whatever fears and doubts rhyme in your beats, surely these would not produce a pleasant rhythm and melody in your life. Go for it. Yesterday you were sixteen, now you are twenty-five, and tomorrow you will be sixty, but you are not even sure if you still have a ticket for tomorrow. There might not be an assurance that everything will be okay, but at least you liberate yourself from self-doubts and fears. The One who lives in you is greater than your fears and doubts. *Genuine faith is trusting the Lord with all your heart, soul, and mind, always leaning in His ways, and trusting His promises, even if you do not know what's next.*

When you choose fear, you give life to unbelief.
When you choose fear, you also numb joy and happiness.
When you choose fear, you stay in the cage of familiarity and mediocrity.
When you choose fear, you accept defeats instead of victories.
When you choose fear, you see darkness instead of light.
When you choose fear, you also miss the great things He prepared for you, the miracles and blessings for those who believe.

Write down your fears and slowly let them go. Then, open your Bible and meditate on His promises.

Day 24: Fallen And Broken

If you feel fallen and broken, read this.

It's okay to admit that you are fallen and broken, longing and inadequate, tempted and weary, insecure and lost. At times, you may feel like hanging on a thread, remaining in the pit of emptiness and loneliness. Sometimes doubts, anxieties, and fears are creeping, and hopes are dying. Unbelief and frustration wake you in the middle of the night. But I hope you always remember there's a power in His name and you can always have as much of Jesus as you want. You can always pour out everything inside because He understands you. He understands every bit of you, no matter how deep the emptiness you feel; come as you are, no more hiding, no more pretending, and no more trying. He sees you, knows you, and cares for you. Just come as you are because in Him nothing is impossible and He can always transpose your story into something meaningful and beautiful. Perhaps, God is peeling all the layers in you that do not define you anymore, those fears, doubts, and unbelief. He is molding you into the person that you are supposed to be so you can grow into His likeness.

Faith is tested and purified amid the wilderness when you are all alone and surrounded by your inimical voice of fears and doubts. It is when you do not have shoulders to lean on and hands to hold; you find yourself in the lows of life with empty hands and a hurting heart. Even if you try to scream and ask for help, no voice comes out until you find yourself murmuring, lamenting, surrendering, kneeling, bowing, lifting your hands, and praising Him again with all your heart, mind, and soul. It is when you feel like sinking deep in your frustration and depression, crying out like Peter to Jesus and humbly saying, "Lord, save me."

List all the victories, answered prayers, and miracles from the past. Remember His love, you are not forgotten beloved. Meditate His Word, and open your Bible.

Day 25: Healing

Healing occurs when you recognize that you are broken and in desperate need of a healer. God can use your brokenness as a testimony. Every detail is a work of God. You may not realize it right once, but as these heartbreaks become testimonies, you will realize that they were all for nothing. When you expose your brokenness to the light, it loses its power because it will never mend or heal if you keep it hidden. You cannot heal yourself; you must constantly rely on Jesus and ask for help from His people.

Living in a flawed world with hurt people who eventually bring pain to others is the norm. Hurting people, they say, injured people. But imagine living in a broken world with healed people, liberated from the shackles of pain, which gradually heal others. Imagine if everyone chose to be healed by God's power and grace through Jesus Christ. How lovely is it to live? People who have been saved and healed by the name of Jesus Christ won't inflict pain anymore.

Acknowledge your pain here then pray for your healing. Open your Bible and seek Jesus.

Day 26: On Brokenness

May you have the courage not to inflict pain on others when you are hurting. May you have the courage not to turn to a terrible one when others cause pain to you. May you end the curse that we are supposed to hurt each other. May you choose courage even if you are in the midst of pain. May you become the person who paints their pain into something beautiful, something you will be proud of, and something that will speak for His glory. When you offer your brokenness to Him, surely He will restore you and turn you into the person you were supposed to be: purposeful, meaningful, and hopeful.

God calls you of His everlasting love amid your shame and brokenness. His love is the only antidote to your suffering. This love has a name; His name is Jesus. And once you consume His love, you will start loving like Jesus, with no terms, no limits, and no conditions, because that's how He loves you. You will start loving others the way He loves you, you will start loving yourself and the way He loves you.

No one can escape brokenness, it is part of our human existence. The bad news is you can't save yourself from the brokenness of this world. The good news is God sent His only begotten Son Jesus Christ. Have you ever wondered how great His love is? When you understand how depth your sins are, truly you will understand how loving and forgiving He is. His love is the antidote to our human brokenness. For God so loved the world, He gave his only Son that so whoever believes in him should not perish but have eternal life. For God did not send his Son into the world to condemn the world, but so that the world might be saved through him. Whoever believes in him is not condemned, but whoever does not believe is condemned already, because he has not believed in the name of the only Son of God. (John 3:16-18)

Pour out your heart. Tell all your brokenness to God.

Day 27: Before You Lose Hope

God understands your heart's desires, your prayers, and even your frustrations. He sometimes allows you to go through sorrow and anguish to remind you that He is the only source of your strength. At times, even if you pray for blessings, He will let you experience emptiness first, reminding you that He is the only One who can give you the fullness of life. And when you pray for a breakthrough, surely He will break you first, crucifixion before the resurrection. Great souls mature through adversity, storms, and seasons of sorrow. Life in Jesus is designed to be victorious, so if you are facing setbacks, God is not yet done with you. Don't lose heart! Those struggles are for nothing.

Have you ever imagined how great God is? He deals with us individually, specifically, and differently. You have a different story and a different path to venture to fulfill His great purpose.

You need to fill the gaps purposely assigned and designed just for you from the beginning. You have different blessings, and may you finally see them with your eyes.

Pray here.

Day 28: Restoration

One day, you will wake up and you will see a beautiful picture of yourself; rejoicing instead of lamenting, celebrating instead of weeping, venturing instead of remaining, loving instead of hating, and forgiving instead of condemning. But no one has a reserved ticket for tomorrow, no one knows what the future holds, so may you have the courage today. Restore your dying hopes, restore your wavering faith, and restore your fainting soul. Bring back the little child who always runs to the Father and longs to be embraced by Him. Bring back the little child who lives by faith rather than sight, who entirely trusts His Father to do immeasurably more than he asks or imagines. Restore the sparkle in your eyes. Bring back the ardent desire to serve Him that has always existed. Bring back your true design in this world, you were not formed for this world but for His glory- for Jesus alone. Restore your relationship with Jesus once again. He never leaves you.

God can give rebirth to your dying hopes.
God can provide doorways to dead ends.
God can do immeasurably things more than you ask or imagine.
Simply because God is God and you are not.

Praise God here.

**Restored
Renewed
Replenished**

*It is easier to love when you are full of love
because when you pour out love
the more* **He fills you.**

Day 29: Kind Love

One day, you will meet the person who will choose to love you in your imperfections and limitations. One day, you will meet the person who will cherish every tiny bit of you and welcome you with a loving embrace. One day, you will smash into someone's soul who will let you experience the genuine love you deserve, who also desires pure intentions and pursues genuine commitment. One day, you will meet someone who will compliment your faith and love for the Lord , who loves Jesus and His ways, who will ignite your heart and mind through His Word, and who will connect deeply with your very soul. You will meet someone who will add meaning, purpose, and value to your life, who will fight with you in prayers, and will walk with you in faith.

Someday someone out there will be your safe haven and your answered prayer and you will look up at heaven and thank God and utter, "This is how Christ loves me; genuine and peaceful."

How beautiful it is to love like Christ, with no conditions, no manipulations, and no pretensions.

How beautiful it is to walk with someone who is Spirit-filled. Imagine your life is filled with kindness, joy, forbearance, goodness, gentleness, faithfulness, patience, and self-control. Who won't say "NO" to this kind of relationship? Seek Jesus first and know His ways until He leads you to the one He created to fill the spaces between your fingers.

Are you praying for someone already? Oh c'mon go and write here.

Mention him or her in your prayers.

(Now it's your turn)

Day 30:_____

*To the men and women in this generation who still believe that
love is waiting and while you are waiting
may these letters and poems warm your soul.*

Someone Out There

I want to believe that you exist.
maybe you are a thousand miles away,
maybe the ocean set us apart,
but I want to believe
there is someone out there like you
on the other side of the world or
maybe you are just on the other side of the wall,
we are just one step apart but barriers hinder us.

And yes I'll be waiting for you
but while I'm waiting
I will be that someone
I will wait courageously and faithfully
in the midst of pressures and tensions
I will be diligent in fulfilling my plans and dreams
I will strive for purity and continually pray for it
I will hope and cling to the beauty of waiting
because waiting for you shows my obedience
to Him, my desire to please God in this season

'cause I know there's someone out there like you
the one that I exactly needed,
my suitable counterpart;
my best buddy, my study buddy
and my journal buddy
and I know someday this prayer will connect us.

On Love

While others write you some letters,
the right one acts upon his words.
While others give you roses,
the right one makes you bloom.
While others admire your breakthrough,
the right one shows up in your breakdown.
While others give you false hopes
and make you doubt,
the right one brings clarity, peace, and assurance.
While others seem right in your eyes,
the right one is right for your soul
and gentle to your being.
While others give you expensive gifts,
offer you limousine rides, and promise you
grandiose visions for the future,
the right one won't lead you to sin
instead lead you to Christ, bring you to the aisle,
and love you until the end.

Can You Faithfully Wait?

I know how much you desire to be pursued,
I know how much you want to be loved,
I know how much you like to meet the one.
But please can you faithfully wait?

I know you've been including,
uttering this in your prayers,
longing and desiring to be an answered prayer.
But please can you prayerfully wait?

Don't take advantage of your youth,
Your vulnerability, strength, and beauty.
You are fearless to do everything
but please take control of your emotions.

Guard your heart and know your limitations,
It's alright to delay all self-gratifications,
Control your desires and wants
And walks towards purity.

You are already loved and pursued
In His hands and His arms
You are greatly appreciated.
So you can gracefully bloom in your season.

Step Back

Let us both step back for a while,
and fulfill our purpose.
Let us honor this season,
Let us give time to know our Creator,
to serve Him wholeheartedly
to enjoy His presence joyfully
and to love Him sincerely.

Until the right time comes,
when the fruit of waiting is already ripe
because the more that we draw closer to Him
the more that He will lead us to one another.

If

If the season is right
and the fruit of waiting is ripe.

If we both see ourselves completely surrender to God
If we finally loosen our grip
on our insecurities, anxieties and fears.

If both of us are fearless and doubtless of His love
can conquer the myriad feelings and emotions of our
own blood.

If we already surpass all the temptations of our youth
visualize our vulnerability,
surrender our lust and live with purity.

If we already keep His promise
and kneel our knees to the cross
living with His commandments

If our souls finally unite as the universe unfolds
even if it's improbable in our own time and space

If He already says, "Go on my child!"

And see you standing still at the edge of the aisle

Can I finally say?
"I'm the missing part of your rib."

Letters For Your Longing Heart

To my future love,

I've realized that waiting is quite a painful process, but I'm waiting for God to answer-the One who understands me better than anyone else, the One who holds the king's heart and, no doubt, yours as well. I may not know your name right now, but I know God knows you from the depths of your existence, and I am at peace with that. I am confident that God will connect us profoundly and powerfully, not to satisfy our desires, but to glorify Him more in our lives. I still believe there is someone out there like you; we may be in different seasons right now, but we are under the same sky, inhaling His grace. And even though we are flawed and imperfect, I still believe God can write our story beautifully and perfectly.

While we are in this season of waiting and longing, I pray that we both seek to delight ourselves in the Lord and let His love transcend to us. I hope and pray that you love Him more than anything else in the world because I know you will love me the way He loves me. I pray that you are a man of faith, ready to overcome your battles through prayer and God's Word, unafraid to pursue your purpose, take the lead, and take a stand

when necessary. I hope to be your answered prayer and you as well. Let us keep our faith in Him. Let's fight in prayers and let His Word be our guiding path toward each other.

I miss you already even though I haven't met you yet. I know you're someone that only God can give. **See you soon, my future love!**

From,

_____

To the ones who is always liked but never pursued,

You are worthy to be pursued, valued, and cherished.

Others may have yelled at you, "You have high walls that are so hard to break." You may feel there is something wrong with you or that you are not attractive or intelligent enough. Perhaps someone told you, "You're too much, and you deserve someone better." You may feel overlooked and unappreciated at times. Or maybe there are days when you sing this song, "I'm the problem, it's me."

A good mentor once told me, "You will never be wrong to the right person; you are always more than enough for them." You don't need to convince them of your worth. You don't need to force and beg for love because the truth is the right person will pursue, value, and cherish you as a woman. The right person will try harder to win your heart. You don't need to compromise your values and beliefs, so never settle for less.

You are going to meet the one- the person who sees your beautiful soul more than your pretty face. The person who calls you beautiful even with your messy hair, puffy eye bags, and pimple marks. The person who holds your hand when you're anxious and afraid. The person who ignites your mind and heart and connects deeply with your very soul. The person who stands beside you when you're shining and even when you're breaking. The person who prays for you even if you don't know. The person God prepares exactly just for you. Take your time- to know Him more, to get along with others and with yourself. Serve while you're young and you will see how blessed you are as a person. Celebrate others' successful relationships and listen to their advice. Celebrate your small wins and celebrate who you're becoming.

So stop contemplating if you are the one who is always liked and never pursued. God is protecting you from heartaches. He knows your prayers and He knows you've been preparing for it. Right now, all you need to do is trust His timing and enjoy your season. Let Jesus be the One first until He leads you to the right one.

Be the person you hope to be with.

To all the good guys who couldn't pursue,

I know you are contented to like her from a distance. You are happy to glance into her eyes for a second. Words miserably fail when she is around. It is hard to tuck your courage and take chances. Perhaps because she's out of your league and improbable to take space in her world and her heart. It seems that she deserves better than what you can offer. It is hard to take steps and move closer to her even though you are so capable of doing it. Perhaps you are anxious about the probabilities and you are not hopeful about the possibilities. Perhaps, it is only your mind that hinders you from trying and taking the first step.

I hope you will have the courage to deviate from the norm that good guys are often referred to as "torpe guys" because you are inherently nice and can always afford to move back and let go of your loved ones, you can afford to keep your feelings sealed just to protect other people's feelings and opinions, and you can afford not to take the lead and give it to others while absorbing all the pain and sorrow.

If you truly like and love the person, pursue her. Pursue her because you don't want to look back in a few days, months, years, or a decade and wonder what could have been. Pursue her because you don't want to think about all the beautiful times you could have with her or the agony of risking and letting go. Pursue her because you can.

I don't want to instill false hope or reassure you that everything will be fine. No, it does not, but I hope you have the guts to believe that you can do things differently and that you will be committed to yourself. I hope you can move closer to the person who inspires and motivates you to become the better version of yourself. You can gaze at her beauty and flaws and dare to say what you've been thinking and praying for the longest time.

And even if she says "No" you still win because you liberate yourself from your self-doubt and finally you are pursuing growth.

To all the good guys out there,

I hope you will have the patience to wait a little more and dare to pursue the woman you've been praying for. Your effort is not in vain. Your desire to serve God first and do your purpose makes you more attractive. I hope you continue breaking the norm that guys aren't faithful and trustworthy. In this time when boundaries don't matter and are neglected, I'm glad you are honoring and protecting the purity of a lady in the same manner that you value your parents.

I hope you continue to prove that chivalry isn't dead; you can still open doors not only to pretty ladies but also to the elderly and even to breastfeeding moms. You can still date and walk at night with pure intentions and motives. You are true to your feelings and words: fighting the temptations in fervent prayers and beating your silent battles with God's word. You take a stand when it's necessary and take the lead in solving problems. You ask council from mature people around you before making decisions.

Your obedience to God brings blessings and rewards as you wait in His time, and by His grace, He will give you the missing part of your ribs- a suitable counterpart and helper. The woman you exactly needed, the woman He has been preparing for you, the woman who is gentle, secure, and at rest in her spirit, and the woman of noble character.

Aren't you praying for this kind of woman?

So right now, be the kind of man for this kind of woman.

And finally, you can say, "Good guys finish well."

Be strong and courageous. You will make it and take heart!

To the ones who still believe in pure intentions,

They say people with pure intentions never win in this era. In this time when cheating is a norm, flirting becomes a hobby, lying becomes too hip, boundaries are not necessary, chastity isn't the priority, and modesty and chivalry seem for royals.

Perhaps, they are right because it's hard to pursue nobility at this age. But if you still believe in pure intentions, beloved you're doing great! If you're doing this not to be liked or to impress, you're doing great!

Pursue it because it is the right thing to do, and it's okay not to fit in and to dare differently. And soon you'll understand you made the right decision. You will reap what you sow. For every cause, there is an effect.

Stand your ground.

Hold on firmly to your values and beliefs. Character is the most underrated elegance at this time. Perhaps because no one is talking about it. You might think everyone values faces, curves, and muscles more than souls but your pure intentions set you apart from others. Your kindness, authenticity, perseverance, and faith make you more attractive.And if you also meet people with pure intentions, keep them because they are hard to find.

Keep in mind, if you keep yourself pure you will be a special utensil for honorable use. You will be ready for the Master to use you for every good work.

To the ones who still believe in genuine commitment,

I hope you prioritize your heart over someone else's eyes. I hope you give the same love to yourself that you are so willing to give to others. I hope you say all the kind words you always hope to hear from others. I hope you nourish your mind and soul with the right amount of patience and warmth. I hope you remember that you are fully known, fully loved, and fully seen by the King of kings. Treasure your heart and give it to the One who is capable of loving it so when He sees the right one for you, you won't worry because He always chooses the best. Surely He will give it to the one capable enough to protect and love its intricaciesMaximize your season, serve while you're young. Enjoy your journey as a single person, love and embrace your inmost being, fill your cup, and nourish yourself. In this time that pursuing romantic relationships seem superficial, finding a partner seems like buying stuff from online shops. May you always raise beyond the norm. May you hope and pray to pursue genuine relationships who desire pure intentions, who is committed for a bigger purpose.

While waiting honor Him, love God with all your heart, mind, and soul. He pursues you. Inhale His grace and live a life that is pleasing to Him. Enjoy your intimate fellowship with God until you realize that His love is more than enough each day. Pursue your purpose for

His glory. Perhaps God is still removing weaknesses, unbelief, and insecurities deep within.

May you testify to the young ones that waiting upon the Lord is the most beautiful thing while praying for a suitable counterpart. He knows the one you exactly need to fulfill His purpose- the one who can be your prayer partner, ministry partner, and life partner and the one who is ready to go to war with you and to fight battles.

And when that person comes, you won't doubt anymore, no question marks, no what-ifs, and no whys because He will give you peace that surpasses understanding. The one He created precisely to fill the gaps between your fingers, someone who will make your burden and baggage lighter, the one who won't complete you but instead will add more meaning, joy, and purpose in your life, the one who can be your safe space in this world full of uncertainties. So leave the soul that always makes you feel hunted because there is so much more ahead of you. Choose to wait and choose to believe. May you testify that there are still men and women in this generation who still desire a genuine commitment and **Christ-centered relationship.**

Keep the faith!

*Liberate yourself from the things that constantly imprison you, flee from them and run with perseverance, courage, faith, love, and hope to the path of life. It may be full of twists and turns but His grace is enough to carry you until you finish the race. You are free from the bondage of sin because His blood covered you when Jesus was crucified and raised from the tomb. True healing comes from **Jesus** only.*

Write a letter to your ten year-old self. Use the space here.

Write a letter to your present self. Use the space here.

Your Safe Haven

Write a letter to your future self. Use the space here.

*Write a letter to your future love or your present love.
Use the space here.*

Write a letter to the ones who cause pain to you.
Use the space here.

Write a letter to the God. Have a heart to heart session with Him. Pour out your heart, mind, and soul. He knows you very well and He embraces your inmost being, He understands you. Just tell Him, what's inside.

*To all dreamers,
ask yourself
why not me?*

*Have a quiet walk,
quiet time and
quiet talk to yourself.*

*Find God
in the quietness,
in stillness
and in the ordinary.*

To my journal buddies,

I write because it liberates me, when I pour out my emotions and put down my thoughts, my heart, and my mind is blank sheet again ready to learn and feel new things. I hope you feel the same as you finish reading this book. I hope and pray you won't be afraid anymore to be yourself, to chase and persevere toward your dreams, and to add meaning to this world as you live. I am beyond grateful because you help me to step out of my cage so I can share the dusty stories of my soul. And I hope it liberates you as well, all your struggles are meant for nothing. Keep in mind, your story doesn't end in defeats so if you are experiencing defeats now, you're halfway to your story, keep writing it with the Great Author.

Take heart!

Grateful,
Merrel Ya

About the Author

Merrel Ya

Meryl A. Villaruel, also known as Merrel Ya, is an educator, storyteller, poet, and blogger. She writes journals, poems, and articles on life, faith, and love on her blog at merrelya.online and at TikTok @merrel.ya. Writing has been her airbag since she was little. Louisa May Alcott inspired her when she was a kid having her first book "Kate Choice." It was a gift she received from Samaritan Purse Operation Christmas Shoebox and through that she fell in love with reading and collecting books and started writing poems and journals and kept them by herself. She always wrote in secret and was afraid to hit the publish button but as she faces adulthood and her faith in Jesus grows deeper, writing journals help her to liberate herself from insecurities, fears, and doubts. She believed that whenever she pours out her emotions and puts down all her thoughts into her journals, her heart and mind turn into blank sheets again ready to learn and feel new things.

She hopes her journals will resonate around the space and transcend to the souls who need them the most to serve as reminders that they are not fighting battles alone and they can always transpose their stories into something beautiful and meaningful whenever they allow the Great Author and the finisher of life Jesus Christ to live with them.

www.ingramcontent.com/pod-product-compliance
Lightning Source LLC
LaVergne TN
LVHW041611070526
838199LV00052B/3084